UNICORNS

By Marty Erickson

The Child's World
childsworld.com

Published by The Child's World®
1980 Lookout Drive • Mankato, MN 56003-1705
800-599-READ • www.childsworld.com

Photographs ©: Ian Luck/Shutterstock Images, cover (unicorn), 1 (unicorn); Shutterstock Images, cover (background), 1–3 (background), 9, 13, 14, 15, 17, 23; Everett Collection/Shutterstock Images, 5; iStockphoto, 6–7, 24; Dima Sid/Shutterstock Images, 10; Carlos Caetano/Shutterstock Images, 16; Flip Nicklin/Minden Pictures/Newscom, 18–19; Arina P. Habich/Shutterstock Images, 20; A. Sontaya/Shutterstock Images, 21

ISBN 9781503849778 (Reinforced Library Binding)
ISBN 9781503850835 (Portable Document Format)
ISBN 9781503851597 (Online Multi-user eBook)
LCCN 2021939644

Printed in the United States of America

Table of CONTENTS

CHAPTER ONE

ROYAL ANIMAL

A girl and her mom walked through the halls of Stirling Castle. Kings and queens of Scotland used to live there. The walls were lined with beautiful **tapestries**. Artists had woven images using thread. The girl gazed at the images. Unicorns were everywhere.

In one, a unicorn sat in a round pen. It was bright white against the green background. Another tapestry showed knights hunting a unicorn. The girl did not like that one very much. But she could still see how much time it took to make the tapestry. The girl and her mother listened to a tour guide. He told them about the history of the castle. They learned that Scotland's national animal is the unicorn.

The unicorn tapestries in Stirling Castle are copies of older works. The original tapestries were made around 1500.

Unicorns look similar to horses, but stories say they have magical powers.

Unicorns are legendary creatures. Unicorns in art look similar to horses. They have long legs and hooves. But unlike horses, a unicorn has a horn.

Throughout history and around the world, people have told stories about unicorns. Over time, some things about unicorns changed. But unicorns continue to capture people's imaginations today.

CHAPTER TWO

HISTORY OF UNICORNS

Stories of unicorns are thousands of years old. Cultures around the world have **myths** about unicorn-like animals. Chinese legends of *qilin* (CHEE-leen) date back to 2700 BC. These unicorn-like animals had body parts from many animals such as horses, deer, and cows. The appearance of a *qilin* was said to predict the birth or death of an important ruler.

Greek stories of unicorns began around 400 BC. A Greek historian said he saw a unicorn in his travels. He described a creature the size of a horse. The animal was many colors. It was described as having a white body, blue eyes, and purple head. A horn grew from the center of its head. The horn had a red tip, black middle, and white base.

A qilin is often called the Chinese unicorn.

The Throne of Denmark (left) was built for the Danish king in the 1600s. It was said to have unicorn horns on it, though the horns are actually from a different type of animal.

In the Middle Ages, unicorns became a symbol of the Christian religion. The Bible includes a creature called *re'em*. This was sometimes **translated** as *unicorn*. Today, *re'em* is usually translated as *wild ox*. In tapestries, many artists used a unicorn as a symbol for Christ.

Rich people wanted to own unicorn horns. Unicorn horns were also called alicorn. Stories said alicorn had magical powers. People believed alicorn was a remedy for poison. It could clean dirty water.

As a result, rulers in Europe wanted objects made of alicorn. They paid large amounts of money for objects that looked like unicorn horns. Traders sold horns from other animals. They told royals the horns were from unicorns. People made **scepters**, cups, and other objects from horns. These objects were said to protect the users from harm.

CHAPTER THREE

PURE WHITE

Over time, descriptions of unicorns became more horselike. Many images show unicorns with thin bodies and legs. Most stories about unicorns describe them with white hair. A unicorn has a flowing **mane** along its neck. Some unicorns are shown with a lion's tail. This is common when shown on a **coat of arms**. Other images show a tail similar to a horse's.

Some stories say that unlike horses, unicorns have cloven hooves. These hooves look similar to a goat's. Cloven hooves are split in the middle. Some images of unicorns also show them with a beard. This is also similar to a goat. Most unicorn stories have one thing in common. A unicorn has a single horn on its forehead. Images often show a spiral horn.

A unicorn often resembles a horse. Sometimes it has features more like those of a goat. But a unicorn always has a horn.

In some stories, unicorns trust women and calm down in their presence.

Myths about unicorns say they are brave. Stories also say it is difficult to catch a unicorn. Knights could not catch a unicorn using weapons or violence. Unicorns were too strong. Stories said unicorns would fight to defend themselves if they had to. Instead, knights had to trick the unicorn. A young woman could calm a unicorn. Sometimes knights and hunters in stories would then attack it. Other times, the woman would tame and keep the unicorn.

CHAPTER FOUR

UNICORNS TODAY

Unicorns do not exist. But many researchers believe other animals inspired stories about unicorns. People made up stories to explain animals they had never seen before.

Researchers believe Greek accounts of unicorns were actually describing the Indian rhinoceros. A rhinoceros, often called a rhino, has four legs and a single horn. Another animal that could have inspired unicorns is the Arabian oryx. This creature is native to the Middle East.

Indian rhinoceros

When an Arabian oryx is viewed from the side, it can look like it has a single horn.

Narwhals are found in Arctic waters.

The unicorn's mythical spiral horn came from a different animal. Narwhals are a type of whale. A narwhal has a tusk that grows out of its skull. Narwhal tusks can be several feet long. A narwhal tusk can look like a unicorn horn.

Viking traders found narwhal horns washed up on beaches. They traded the horns with Europeans. The Europeans had never seen a narwhal. They believed the tusks were unicorn horns. Some of these tusks are still on display in castles.

Unicorns are a popular theme for parties, pool floats, clothing, and more.

Stories of unicorns continue to hold people's imaginations. Books, TV shows, and movies about unicorns come out every year. *My Little Pony*, *Adventure Time*, and the Pokémon series are all examples. Unicorns in these shows are often brave. Unicorn stories from more than 500 years ago continue to affect how unicorns are described in today's stories.

There are unicorn characters in My Little Pony, *which is a line of toys, movies, TV shows, and more.*

GLOSSARY

coat of arms (KOHT UV ARMZ) A coat of arms is a group of pictures or symbols that represent a person or family. When a unicorn is shown on a coat of arms, it often has a lion's tail.

mane (MAYN) A mane is the long hair that grows on a horse's head and neck. A unicorn is often shown as having a long mane.

myths (MITHSS) Myths are stories told about imaginary creatures or events. There are many myths about unicorns.

scepters (SEP-tuhrs) Scepters are long rods that kings and queens carry. Kings and queens wanted scepters made out of alicorn.

tapestries (TAP-uh-strees) Tapestries are woven images that hang on walls. Tapestries at Stirling Castle show unicorns.

translated (TRANS-lay-tuhd) To have translated something is to have changed words from one language into another. *Re'em* has been translated as *unicorn* and as *wild ox*.

Viking (VY-king) A Viking was a warrior or trader from northern Europe who lived from approximately 800 to 1000 AD. Viking traders found narwhal tusks on Arctic beaches.

TO LEARN MORE

In the Library

Alberti, Theresa Jarosz, and Sara Cucini. *Unicorns.* New York, NY: AV2 by Weigl, 2020.

Jeffrey, Gary. *Unicorns.* New York, NY: Gareth Stevens Publishing, 2012.

Klepeis, Alicia Z. *Scotland.* Minneapolis, MN: Bellwether Media, 2020.

On the Web

Visit our website for links about unicorns:

childsworld.com/links

Note to Parents, Teachers, and Librarians: We routinely verify our Web links to make sure they are safe and active sites. So encourage your readers to check them out!

INDEX

ABOUT THE AUTHOR

Marty Erickson is a writer living in Minnesota. They write books for young people full time and like to go hiking.